Structures of the Heart

Amber DeVan

BookLeaf Publishing

Presentation by *BookLeaf Publishing*

Web: www.bookleafpub.com

E-mail: info@bookleafpub.com

ISBN: 9789357745253

First edition 2023

To my childhood self, you did it kid.

ACKNOWLEDGEMENT

First and foremost, I would like to thank my parents John & Juana for always supporting my endeavors no matter how far off the beaten path I venture. I owe my entire existence to you, I definitely hit the parent jackpot. To my friends who have become my lifeblood, I cannot imagine my life without you. Here's to those long-awaited hangouts that I have put on hold! Finally, to my partner in crime, I am so grateful the universe saw fit to have our paths cross. Same team, always.

Within

Dreams of my existence
Solely in itself

And yet I,
Graceful and overflowing with energy

Ramble on living within my
Own heart and soul

Pieces

old sorrows aching
piercing the stillness within
broke reality

Ode to Night

Wondrous Night!
Lit by moonlight,
Has brought forth my shade again.
He hears my plea
And comes to me
To guide me through worlds foreign.

The moon's full beams
Carried my dreams
To find this shadow akin.
As only he
Can awaken me
And steal me far from within.

I'd prayed before,
But nevermore.
I'd feared I'd been forsaken.
To wander Earth
Repressed from mirth
Life: lonely, sad, and barren.

Then he came 'round
Without a sound
Beckoning me with a grin.
Alas! Twas he
Who finally
Gave reprieve from all the sin.

A Presence

5

See me.

As I am.

A piece of the world.

A proof of life.

All is not chaos,

Nor is it forgotten.

Warmth

6

I was disagreeable by instinct,
    but immensely vivacious.

The great difference,
    a matter of difficulty.
Increasingly unfavorable;
    and somewhat burdensome.

I could not restrain myself.

Fervor has become my light in the darkness.

Prowess

These gentlemen
She vanquished them
Years before
Her sweetheart
Would marry her

Stolen Moments

Frozen in time
a moment passed
but still unpassable
vast instances
created once
thought unforgettable

uniquely deemed
greatly cherished
even regrettable
spoken aloud
only one word,
Unimaginable.

And Again

Breathless.
Unrelenting.

Swept up in the occurrence of it all.

Finding one's self, bending and flowing;
to meet another's form.

Distracted.
Blinded.

Falling from where once stood a ledge.

Seeking shelter from consciousness and dread.
Unearthing sharpened instincts.

Challenged.
Changed.

Solace in seclusion, calm and tranquility.
Until the next venture comes to blend.

Ahead

I set about leaving him all alone, grumbling:
"Woe is me!"

I look around... I'm alive.

This is the last he'll ever have.

It is time to move along.

The path ahead black and endless.

I go out like hungry wolves in the desert.

Unbalanced.
Delirious.
Awake.

Alone

loneliness lingered
disdainfully holding tight
although I endured

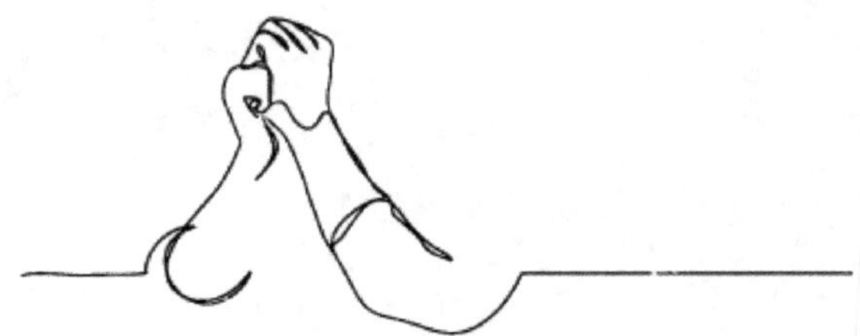

Try Harder

12

I had fallen asleep with eyes wide open.

Tired and over-excited at the same time.

Only dawn made sense.

I was resisting.

Living through my execution.

Keep. Going.

I felt tired and
whenever I tried
rifles aimed at me
I was resisting; imploring
for the last dawn

I didn't want
my past life and the kinds of things that had
happened
I wanted to liberate myself
and my life before me was not finished
it was only an outline

Forward

outliving my chance
no longer weeping from fear
sudden strong relief

Manifestation

I never dreamed so deeply;
but what can one do all alone
surrounded by nothing but falling stars?
And as the stars fell, I smiled sweetly.
Wait… tomorrow I will find you.

A Gem

Solitary grandeur rose and followed her.
The ends of the earth
seeming like mere steps.

Beneath her confident stride,
accompanied by simplicity.
Grace and ease guiding her path.

Her charm alluring for many,
especially by those in search of adventure.

Z

He himself escaped.
Bound for starry dartings over dust.

The towns.
The ports.

Preaching more simply his prodigious
restlessness.
Around the curves of the country
his soul's dilemma shifted,
straightening.

A sense of the struggle, blinded.

And I let him live here.

Cohorts

Together as one through experiences, past
and present.

Transcendence with elegant imperfection.

Form a bond unknown to outsiders.

Built to last and exceed expectations.

Its duo forever changed by wonderful, sweet
luck.

Glowing

In dizziness of the heart's sudden descent.

Limitless madness among my soul.

All tingling without thought.

Suddenly desire.

Then a rushing, full swoon all that enabled me.

Harmony

Adoration stole nightly quarrels
the sound of stillness, a hymn.
A cry for relief, for rest, for sleep.
To be rid of intolerable aching.
To see nothing and think of nothing.
To stroll along the broad horizon,
Voyaging calmly into solidarity.

Tethered

21

their gaze remained locked
and they collapsed together
large successive swallows
gulping in the fresh air

feeling all emotion
they were normal, healthy
deeply feeling good
his mouth arrived home on her mouth
the sight was beautiful

Sans Regret

without question
the dream remains
our love affair
connections to commitment

these small fragments
one by sweet one
shape every memory
Handsomely